writers' awards 2000

THE **ARTS COUNCIL** OF ENGLAND

ISBN 0-7287-0803-5

Author photographs by Pete Jones except Paul Farley (Jane Bown) and Mick Imlah
Designed and typeset by Ned Hoste/2H
Printed by BSC Print

Contents

Introduction

Established in 1965, The Arts Council of England Writers' Awards are unique among literary prizes, buying time for a writer to finish their current work-in-progress. The applications are judged anonymously; awarded by writers to writers.

The age of the winners varies considerably; some already have a formidable reputation and have written many books, but due to a lack of financial support, regular income and, indeed, the cost of researching their books, may still need a cash injection to be able to complete their next work. Some winners are younger writers, who find that the boost of winning an award means they are able to launch their careers.

Over the past 35 years, the Writers' Awards have been effective in encouraging and supporting a strong creative, literary force in this country. Past winners have included Graham Swift, Ian McEwan, A.S.Byatt, V.S.Naipaul, Hugo Williams and Carol Ann Duffy. Salman Rushdie's *Midnight's Children* was also written with the assistance of an award. As a direct result of winning a Writers' Award, David Almond was able to concentrate on his writing full time and, in 1998, won the Whitbread Award for Children's Literature with *Skellig*.

This year's Writers' Awards were judged by Andrew Motion, Anne Fine and Alan Hollinghurst. This book features extracts from the fifteen winning writers' works-in-progress.

Hilary Mantel

"... writers who venture abroad must always travel first class and stay at the best hotels. Otherwise, they encounter hazards and hardships, write very dull books about them, and become a burden to the spirit."

David Almond

David Almond lives in Newcastle upon Tyne, was a teacher, and has published books for adults and children. He has had many stories broadcast on Radio 4 and published in magazines and anthologies. He won a Writers' Award for *Kit's Wilderness* in 1998 (now published by Hodder) and a Whitbread Award for Children's Literature for *Skellig*. *Counting Stars* will be published in September.

My award came in 1998. I'd already been writing for years. My first story was published in 1979 in the late lamented IRON magazine. It was the first of many to appear in the kind of magazines that are so important to a healthy literary culture: Stand, Edinburgh Review, London Magazine, Sunk Island Review, The Echo Room... Writing short stories is hardly the fast route to success, so I always knew I was in for the long term. I worked as a teacher, writing in evenings and holidays. At one point, I gave up the day job, eked out a few hundred pounds while I lived in a Norfolk commune, writing in a dilapidated and beautiful mansion. I ran out of cash, returned to teaching with the completed manuscript of my first short story collection, *Sleepless Nights*, published by Iron Press in

1985. It came out to a squeak of acclaim and a vast amount of silence.

In 1987 I became editor of the fiction magazine, Panurge, a labour of love and madness that lasted six years. Now teaching full-time again, I also began a novel, *Seances*. It helped me find an agent, Maggie Noach, an angel who would encourage me and stick by me for years before she earned a single penny. *Seances* went to 33 publishers, and was rejected by them all. I took a deep breath, passed Panurge back to its founding editor, John Murray, and began again. Stories continued to appear in the magazines. I started another. Halfway through, I walked into a bookshop and felt envy and spite for the writers whose books packed the shelves. Bitterness. I'd seen enough of bitter writers, and I didn't intend to join their ranks. I went back to the heart of my world. I wrote a series of stories about my childhood, about the people and places I'd grown with. Paradoxically, these little half-real, half-imaginary tales of events in a small Tyneside town, brought me my biggest audience yet: Radio 4, prestigious magazines, a number of prizes. I called the collection *Counting Stars*, addressed it to Maggie, dropped it into the post box, walked away, and the first line of a new story appeared in my head: "I found him in the garage on a Sunday afternoon."

This new story came with great speed and urgency. At times, it almost wrote itself. I knew that it was a novel for children - an audience whose minds are fluid, able to accept all kinds of possibilities - and that I was writing better than I ever had before. In writing it, I learned a huge amount about the ways of the imagination and the elemental nature of storytelling. The story seemed to come from nowhere, but at the end, looking back, I saw that it had been prepared for by the stories about my own childhood, and by the years of work attending to language and narrative. The book was called *Skellig*. Maggie said it would win prizes. Hodder took it straight away and said it would be published all around the world. I took it all with a pinch of salt and set off on a new book, *Kit's Wilderness*, another children's novel, commissioned by Hodder, that I was determined to finish before *Skellig* was published.

Where *Skellig* had been like writing in a dream, this book was like struggling with a nightmare. I wrote and rewrote the beginning many times, and wondered whether I would ever bring it to life. But this really was a time of gifts. The childhood stories won me a Hawthornden Fellowship: a month in a Scottish castle with nothing to do but focus on my work. I arranged leave from work. I read that one of the Arts Council Writers' Awards was to be for a children's writer. At the castle, I wrote the first third of the book and submitted it for an award. I won the award. In all the years of writing, there couldn't have been a better time for this to happen. I knew exactly what I needed to do. I arranged more unpaid leave, almost six months this time. I completed *Kit's Wilderness*. I put together the first notes for another novel, *Heaven Eyes*. During the leave, *Skellig* was published, and had to be reprinted within days. Rights were sold around the world. It was shortlisted for The Whitbread. Reviews were stunning. People began to ask how I would follow *Skellig*'s success. With *Kit's Wilderness*, I was able to say, and thanks to the Arts Council I've already been able to finish it.

Now, two years after I won my wonderful award, I'm no longer teaching, and I'm on my way to making a living from my books. *Kit's Wilderness* is now winning prizes, *Heaven Eyes* has come out. *Counting Stars* will be published in September. After the long slow haul that I expected, things are happening quickly.

The Arts Council Writers' Award came at a crucial time, and helped me complete that crucial second book. I'll be eternally grateful.

Martina Evans

Martina Evans was born in 1961 and grew up in County Cork. She trained as a radiographer in St Vincent's hospital, Dublin, and moved to London in 1988. She has published two novels and her second collection of poetry, *All Alcoholics are Charmers,* was published in 1998 by Anvil. Her latest novel, *No Drinking, No Dancing, No Doctors,* for which she won a Writers' Award in 1999, is now published by Bloomsbury.

Until I was thirty four years of age and won a Betty Trask award, the only thing I had ever won was a holy picture in a school raffle. The nun in charge of study saw me making a disgusted face when the prize was announced and I got a lecture on ingratitude and disrespect along with my holy picture when I went up to collect it from Mother Brendan. I returned to my seat feeling very sorry for myself. All the other girls got colouring books; was there ever such an unlucky person?

In 1993, I had been writing for less than three years when I was short-listed for a Sunday Tribune/Hennessey Award. The awards were held on a weekday and as I had no holidays left, I had to approach my boss, the Superintendent Radiographer at the Whittington hospital. I explained to him that I needed the day off to go to a reception in Dublin. The Superintendent Radiographer was amazed to hear that I wrote poetry and he was full sure that I was going to win. Why else would they be flying me over? Soon the whole X-ray Department found out that I wrote poetry: 'We never realised you were so romantic!' they said. And they, too, were all absolutely sure I was going to win the prize of one thousand pounds. The thrill of being short-listed evaporated as I flew off to Dublin, desperate to win. How was I going to face everyone if I flew back without the prize?

I flew back without the prize.

I applied for three years before I won the Arts Council Writers' Award in 1999 and it is one of the best things that ever happened to me. After ten years of struggle with my writing, I no longer thought in terms of luck: I felt recognised and supported when I got that award.

Support is the single most important thing for a writer. It is not just the money, it is the fact that the writing itself is valued.

Until 1996, I worked as a radiographer. Trying to do two jobs while minding a young child was extremely hard work and I became ill as a result. The writing was not as good as it could have been. A two-book deal had allowed me to give up work and then, for the first time in my life, I was without a steady salary. Despite publishing two novels and two books of poetry, I never received any royalty cheques. Money became very scarce, yet I felt I was writing properly for the first time in my life and I needed time.

Novels or books of poems cannot be rushed. They need to grow properly. My first three books were rushed and they were written at the end of a hard working day when I was dead on my feet. Now I dropped my daughter off to school and came home to write. I was fresh, my head was clear, I felt I was really writing but I was earning scarcely anything. I couldn't understand the royalty statements that arrived every six months with minus signs at the bottom. Was I ever going to get any money? An agent told me not to expect much, after all I hadn't written *Captain Corelli's Mandolin.*

Well, I didn't need to be reminded that I hadn't written *Captain Corelli's Mandolin* but I was wondering if I needed to go back to radiography. I knew that my writing would suffer and that my daughter would hate having a childminder. It was a very stressful time. But then I got the Arts Council Writers' Award and the stress just rolled away. I had the time and the money to finish a book properly for the first time in my life. *No Drinking, No Dancing, No Doctors* was published by Bloomsbury in March 2000.

Michael Holroyd

"What we need are more readers, not more authors."

Elizabeth Barrett

Elizabeth Barrett is currently working on her second collection of poetry, *The Bat Detector.* Her first collection, *Walking on Tiptoe,* won the Staple First Editions Award in 1998. The recipient of a Yorkshire and Humberside Arts Bursary (1996), her work has been widely published in magazines. She will co-edit Staple Magazine from 2001.

From THE BAT DETECTOR

RINGING THEIR LOVED ONES

1

The ethereal chill of silence
and sky darkening unnaturally
lasted only a couple of minutes.
What surprised me, afterwards,
was how quickly things became usual
again - the way normality restored itself,
as if nothing had happened.
That evening, in the ordinary dusk,
when I tried to use my mobile phone
the display read *network overloaded.*
The guy on the helpline explained
all the lines were jammed by people
talking about this extraordinary thing -
how everyone was ringing their loved ones.

11

A couple of months after the eclipse,
news one morning of an incident:
how the sky over west London was darkening
as burning carriages and flaming tracks
belched black smoke from the crash;
how the two commuter trains had been packed;
how passengers were still trapped.
Next day, scenes on TV of tangle and scorch
and a debris of things which didn't belong
anymore (a photo, briefcase, cardigan).
And the silence disturbed only by this:
mobile phones going off, incessantly,
amid the wreckage - people praying for news,
ringing and ringing their loved ones.

THE MAN WHO HATED THE SUN

has an array of hats.
Once owned, simply, a navy beret
but chooses, now, between
Panama, Tarboosh and Kepi,

hunts for small-sized versions
to coax their child: hoods and cloaks
the hair growing its fearful camomile
in deadly blond image of her.

Hot days, ties bandeaux around their heads:
secures the cotton squares tight
across their temples, knots them firmly
at the nape of their necks,

remembering how the chocolate clot
bunched, slid its twisting tissue,
smooth and sparkling as a precious gem,
to mole through the left side of her head.

Sits with the child in a darkened room,
absorbed by sepia tints: the walls stained
with umbers, terracottas - their cool cave
banishing light from their days.

BLACKBIRD

I have broken things down, simply:
with the patience of one hundred pictures,
the silent scribe of my hands in air;
through the range of my voice,
the tableaux of gesture and mime,
I have repeated them again and again.
Today, after twenty two weeks
of trying to teach him that two follows
one, how to curl his fingers
round a pen and shape his lips to oo
and mm, he sits at the table rocking;
dangles his hands before his face,
eyes glazed, while I cry.

Perhaps we will call it a day -
go out back to where the blackbird
is sounding the urgent tchich tchich tchich
of her alarm, keeping our cat at bay -
defending her nestlings from a horror
she did not conceive of when eggs were laid.
It is her persistence I admire;
the way she never lets up.
How fearless she is, upon the fence,
prepared to risk a pounce's breath
to protect her birds before they fly.
She knows how to live the slim chance;
instinct unswayed by poor odds, the long shot.

Elizabeth Barrett

UPSIDE DOWN

I weigh plus and minus
from the window bay of this room:
wait, in a wide glance of sky,
stark verdict on the evens test
I can't affect: the 50:50 chance
to fail (or pass) without a try.
The only sway I owned -
whether or not to know.

Under the blown silk curve
of belling sky, this wash of blue,
recollect a day I didn't mean to know.
How, across a surgery's reception hatch,
I picked from scattered index cards
urgent words inked in red:
HIV+ (to come in)
and walked home wondering who.

No surprise in this: thin men there
were passing tapestry with gulls, pier lights,
distant ships: temporary beneath the high stretch
of sea to sky, that wide blue fix.
What bothered me was casually knowing it:
that a phone would ring; disturb the stillness
of his morning bath - the suds bursting and crackling
around forgotten amber, the soap dissolving.

And wonder, now, where my card waits -
whether, momentarily, it will attract the eye
of receptionist, passing visitor to the ward;
if someone will decipher, across a shoulder,
from wrong side of a desk: ꓯWONIƆꓤꓯƆ
 - that casual knowing while I still lie in either/or;
this calm before my world
could turn itself upside down.

Francesca Clementis

Francesca Clementis was born in London in 1958. Her first novel, *Big Girls Don't Cry*, was published by Piatkus in 1999. Her second novel, *Mad About The Girls*, submitted while in progress for the Arts Council Writers' Awards, has recently been finished and will be published by Piatkus in September 2000. She is currently working on her third novel.

From MAD ABOUT THE GIRLS

A challenge: I give you the story of my life in under 100 words. You have to guess what comes next. Pay attention.

1) Born 36 years ago to a wonderful mother and devoted father - or so I was told. I was handed over to a different mother and father five days later.

2) Didn't get into grammar school of my choice. Went to local comprehensive where rolling tobacco was most popular product in tuck shop.

3) Didn't get good enough A-levels for Cambridge. Went to Sussex University. (Watch for the clues, they're not subtle...)
4) Dreamed of becoming a magician. Became a teacher.
5) Wanted husband and four children.
6) Happily settled for ten years with husband and four children - now you supply the tag...
What did you guess? Something on the thwarted dream theme, of course. After all, I gave you enough pointers. So what did you come up with? Someone dying, husband betraying me, leaving me, kids turning out badly, disfiguring illness, miscarriage of justice landing me in prison? Good suggestions, all perfectly plausible, all wrong. I'm fine. Husband and kids are all fine. All healthy, all happy, all well-adjusted. It's just that they are actually somebody else's husband and somebody else's children.

And that somebody else wants them back.

"You should have known this would happen sooner or later!" you scream from the Dress Circle. But don't be too quick to heap scorn on me for being the author of my own circumstances. The outcome of the choices I made ten years ago may appear to be more dramatic than your average suburban saga, but am I the only person who's dared to hope that she might beat the odds, buck the trends, win the prize?

I know how easy it is to spot behaviour patterns in somebody else's life. God, I do it all the time, anything to take my mind off my own mistakes. Speaking of which, let's take a look at you. When was your first time? You know what I'm talking about. That first stab of panic when you looked ahead towards your dream or your goal or your destiny and it wasn't there. It wasn't in front of you because it was behind you or over there or anywhere else except where it was supposed to be.

And dreams are the whole point, aren't they, the arrowhead on the shaft? They give you direction, purpose, meaning. If we didn't have something to aim for, we'd all be flitting in and out of parallel lives, toying randomly with hobbies, careers and partners. Well we all know what happened to my dreams, so let's look at yours. Please. Indulge me. Humour me. Don't let me carry the banner of female fallibility all by myself here. How did you lose sight of *your* goals, the original authentic ones, not the ones you've tweaked to fit your present situation?

It started early, didn't it? When you longed to be Mary in the nativity play but were cast as fifth sheep; when you asked Father Christmas for a Sindy doll and you got an encyclopaedia; when you asked for a piano and got a stylophone - a second-hand one without Rolf Harris's accompanying instruction booklet. And thus the pattern was forged.

You were going to marry in white in a pretty village church when you were 21, weren't you? To a man who looked like David Cassidy (my own choice - insert pop icon appropriate to your personal era), was sensitive, faithful, wrote and read poetry, was also a promising executive with a car, a flat and a mother who lived at least 300 miles away. You actually got married, when? Were you 31 or even 41? Did you wear green? It was probably in a registry office in a new town civic centre and you had to pretend that you didn't mind, really, and white weddings are just silly teenage fantasies. And no, of course you didn't want a lot of fuss. And your husband? A nice man, I've no doubt but...but...

So how could it have happened? Where did that dream disappear to? Somewhere along your squiggly lifeline you'd meandered off and settled for second-best. Or sixtieth-best. Whatever. And you didn't mean to. Nobody does. Pink bedrooms all over the world are full of little girls dreaming of being ballet dancers who will end up becoming aromatherapists. Or maybe there are children who dream of being aromatherapists. There's a scary thought for our new millennium.

Andrew Crumey

Andrew Crumey was born in Glasgow in 1961. His novels are *Music, In A Foreign Language, Pfitz, Mr Mee* and *D'Alembert's Principle* (Dedalus). *Impossible Tales* is his work in progress. He lives in Newcastle upon Tyne.

From IMPOSSIBLE TALES

For a long time Robbie Coyle used to wet the bed. At last his exasperated mother decided they should see the doctor, who listened patiently to her explanation, then turned to Robbie. "Do you have bad dreams?"

"Sometimes," Robbie admitted.

"Do you play sport?"

Robbie said he liked playing at space ships. He wanted to be an astronaut when he grew up.

"What sort of things do you read? Stories, comics? Not these awful American things, I hope."

Robbie didn't know quite what the doctor had in mind, so he showed him the Look And Learn his mother had bought for the occasion and this was declared healthy enough. The doctor addressed Mrs Coyle again.

"Your son strikes me as a nervous lad, though not excessively so. But he's bright for a nine-year old, and that's the real problem. He's got a vivid imagination, frets too much. What he needs is fresh air, an interest, good reading. Have you ever heard of Walter Scott?" he said to Robbie, who shook his head solemnly. "Try *Ivanhoe*, that's a fine story. I read it when I was your age."

They left the surgery and went straight to the public library where Robbie was registered with the same silent formality that had marked his encounter with the local health authority. Mrs Coyle then hunted among shelves as crammed as a chemist's drugs counter while Robbie pulled down something called *Rocket to the Stars*.

Mrs Coyle couldn't find *Ivanhoe*. Robbie, sitting on the floor with musty books towering over him, peered round the end of the bookcase and saw her go to the desk.

"I can put it on order for you," said the assistant.

"Actually," said Mrs Coyle, "I just want something that'll stop him wetting the bed."

"Oh," said the assistant. "Well, you could try *Kidnapped*, I suppose."

As soon as they got home Robbie started reading

Kidnapped and found it the most boring thing in the universe. There weren't even any pictures. *Rocket to the Stars* had a V2 painted like a chequer-board, and a monkey in a space suit, and loads of other things. But his mother and the assistant had both agreed that if anything was going to make him wee the bed it was stuff like that. Instead he was allowed *The Boys' Book Of Facts*. Next morning his bed was wet again.

Robbie hoped his condition would improve before he grew up and applied to be an astronaut. *The Boys' Book of Facts*, in its "careers" section, declared that astronauts needed excellent powers of concentration and a cool head. Peeing the bed wasn't specified as a cause of automatic disqualification, and Robbie would of course point out to the selection panel that a small bag within an astronaut's pressurised suit is there to collect every weightless drop of urine passed while waking or asleep; nevertheless he knew it made him look like someone whose head was far from cool, since in all his comics not a single hero had ever woken to find his mattress soaked through every intervening layer of bed-sheet and folded towel, all because he had a drink after seven o'clock the night before.

The problem was that he had a vivid imagination. His mum said this meant he spent too long in his own thoughts instead of going out and playing.

The word sounded like a cross between "livid", which meant very angry, and "Vivian", who worked at the baker's and was very fat and always telling jokes. Vivid was a state that lay somewhere in between, though since Robbie was unsure quite where, his condition appeared insoluble.

A man on television gave advice to children wanting to go into space, saying they must first work as US Air Force test pilots. Robbie told his dad; Mr Coyle lowered his newspaper, looked disapprovingly at his son and said, "You'd end up in Vietnam."

In that case, Robbie countered, he'd be a Soviet cosmonaut.

"You don't speak Russian."

"I'll learn."

He persuaded his mum to take him back to the library, where Mrs Coyle, her faith in medical science having been shattered by the failure of the doctor's prescription, now allowed Robbie to exchange *Kidnapped* and *The Boys' Book Of Facts* for *Russian In One Month* and *Military Aircraft 1958*. The woman at the desk eyed him with some incredulity as he checked them out. "He's going to be an astronaut," Mrs Coyle explained.

Bernardine Evaristo

Bernardine Evaristo is a Londoner. *The Emperor's Babe* (Penguin/Hamish Hamilton, Spring 2001) recreates the decadent world of Roman London through its feisty protagonist, Zuleika. Bernardine's novel-in-verse, *Lara,* (Angela Royal Publishing 1997) won the first *EMMA Best Novel Award* in 1999 and was a *Daily Telegraph* and *New Statesman* Book of the Year.

From THE EMPEROR'S BABE, a novel-in-verse.

Amo Amas Amat

Who do you love? Who *do* you love?
When the man you married goes off

for months on end, quelling rebellions
at the frontiers, or playing hot-shot senator in Rome;

his flashy villa on the Palatine Hill, home
to another woman, I hear,

one who has borne him offspring.
My days are spent managing this house,

its vast mosaic walls full of the scenes on Olympus,
for my husband loves melodrama.

They say his mistress is an actress,
a flaxen-fraulein type, from Germania Superior.

Oh everyone envied me, *La Bella Negreeta!*
born in the back of a shop on Gracechurch Street,

who got hitched to a Roman nobleman,
whose parents sailed out of Khartoum on a barge,

not a burnished throne, its poop of beaten gold
but packed with vomiting brats,

and cows releasing warm turds
onto their bare feet. Thus perfumed,

they made it to Londinium on a donkey,
with only a thin purse and a fat dream.

Dad wandered the streets looking for work,
but there was no room at the inn

so he set up shop on the kerb
and sold sweet cakes which Mum made.

(He's told me this story a *mille* times.)
Now he owns several shops, selling everything

from vino to shoes, veggies to tools,
and he employs all sorts to work in them,

a Syrian, Libyan, Jew, Persian,
hopefuls just off the olive barge from Gaul,

in fact anyone who'll work for pebbles.
When Felix came after me, Dad was in ecstasy,

Father-in-law to Lucius Aurelius Felix, no less.
I was spotted at the baths of Cheapside,

just budding, and my fate was sealed,
to a man thrice my age, and thrice my girth -

all at sweet thirteen, even then Dad
thought I was getting past it.

So, I was sent off to a snooty Roman bitch
called Clarissa for decorum classes,

learnt how to talk, eat and fart,
how to get my amo amas amat right, and ditch

my second generation plebby creole.

Zuleika accepta est.
Zuleika delicata est.
Zuleika bloody goody-two shoes est.

But I dreamt of creating mosaics,
of remaking my town with bright stones and glass.

But no! Numquam! It's not allowed.
Sure, Felix brings me presents, when he deigns

to come west. I've had Chinese silk, a marble
figurine from Turkey, gold earrings
shaped like dolphins and I have the deepest
fondness for my husband of course,

sort of, though he spills over me like dough
and I'm tempted to call Cook mid-coitus

to come trim his sides so that he fits me.
Then it's puff and *Ciao Baby!*

Solitudoh, solitudee, solitudargh!

Simon Armitage

"... I've always found it useful not to see writing as a career, but to think of it instead as stolen time or a kind of luxury."

Paul Farley

Paul Farley was born in Liverpool in 1965, and studied at the Chelsea School of Art. His first collection, *The Boy from the Chemist is Here to See You* (Picador), won a Forward Prize in 1998 and was shortlisted for the Whitbread Poetry Award. In 1999 he received a Somerset Maugham award and was named Sunday Times Young Writer of the Year. *Windowlickers* is his work in progress.

From WINDOWLICKERS

FROM A WEEKEND FIRST

One for the money. Arrangements in green and grey
from the window of an empty dining-car.
No takers for this Burgundy today
apart from me. I'll raise a weighted stem
to my homeland scattering by, be grateful for
these easy-on-the-eye, Army & Navy
surplus camouflage colours that seem
to mask all trace of life and industry;
a draft for the hidden dead, our forefathers,
the landfills of the mind where they turned in

with the plush and orange peel of yesteryear,
used up and entertained and put to bed
at last; to this view where everything seems to turn
on the middle distance. Crematoria, multiplex
way stations in the form of big sheds
that house their promises of goods and sex;
to the promise of a university town,
its spires and playing fields. No border guards
will board at this station, no shakedown
relieve me of papers or contraband:
this is *England*. Nobody will pull the cord
on these thoughts, though the cutlery and glasses
set for dinner are tinkling at a bend,
a carriage full of ghosts taking their places.

Now drink to slow outskirts, the colour wheels
of fifty years collected in windows;
to worlds of interiors, to credit deals
with nothing to pay until next year, postcodes
where water hardens then softens, where rows
of streetlights become the dominant motif
as day drains, and I see myself transposed
onto the dark, lifting my glass. Belief
is one thing, though the dead have none of it.
What would they make of me? This pinot noir
on my expenses, time enough to write
this on a Virgin antimacassar –

the miles of feint, the months of Sunday school,
the gallons of free milk, all led to here:
an empty dining-car, a single fool
reflected endlessly on the night air.

JOSEPH BEUYS

To write about elemental things, to render
the world in its simpler smells and shapes and textures,
to describe how tallow collects under the finger-

nails, how felt feels against bare skin
is not, I repeat, not an option
having lived several times removed from the world as itself,

although it can do no harm to imagine
myself as the stricken airman
carted indoors by the local women

who'd take it in turns attending to the matter
of rubbing in the *Stork SB* and *Flora*,
the *Golden Churn* and *I Can't Believe It's Not Butter*.

FLY

Hardly anything, a fine-winged fly on the window pane,
one of the day's ten-thousand seconds captured,
made visible. Inconsequential, its moments in the world
squandered on this wall of light it can't surmount,

far from water. It must have got in overnight
through one of those chinks we don't like to admit
to owning – with our campaigns of strip-blinds,
insect-o-cutors
and arsenic paper, you could say we haven't got on,

that you remind us of something we'd rather forget;
some thread of trial and error, intricate
and long since perfected, fully working before we arrived
on the scene at one minute to midnight; that you knew

summers of the smaller hours, Venusian seasons
and still go through the whole thing on bus shelter roofs,
canals, anywhere warm or wet enough. Can you see me
fly; a castellated, bloodshot eye, day's growth

and did you see me enter, or feel the slammed air
then a settling through the house, silence again
and onwards in your slow ascent from the sill
against the dawn's skin, gorged a red that you see in waves.

Up close, you've spat on your hands, that same solving rub
when faced with sashes, great bays, or top decks of buses
the world over, baffled in our era of glass
that you slip against time and again, en route for an edge

though it's strange the way you'll so readily accept a frame,
tracing an algebra of infinite confinement,
a treatise on the lack of straight lines in nature,
that hard bitten philosophy found in cage birds

and aquaria; a pattern I've seen displayed
on skylights, shithouse walls, the pelts of dead dogs;
or trapped in famine footage, a matte blip
that kept Lindbergh awake as he crossed the Atlantic

again in the late film. The east has grown bright.
In your register of time, I have held my pen
steadily for hours. In mine, all I have to say
is brushed to one side as I give up writing this,

take a fly-age to cross the room, draw back the lace;
to lift up the latch, encourage you with one sharp breath,
the air catching your wings, letting noun become verb,
and you join the world of things, of everything being the case.

Don Paterson

"Good artists don't
have to broaden
their experience.
They make things up.
When Delacroix
wanted to paint a
tiger, he used his cat
as a model and made
it big and stripy;
it turned out
pretty well."

Christopher Firth

Christopher Firth had a novel, *Miasma*, published by Springboard in 1997. He has had short stories published in collections and literary magazines, including five of the *Electraglade Tales*, from which the 'Walls' extract is taken. Recently, he edited a short story collection, *The Unexpected Pond*, for Route\YAC publishers. *Hocus Pocus Hullabaloo*, a collection of short bizarre stories for younger readers, is published by Solomon Press at Easter 2000. He is currently completing the *Electraglade Tales* and working on a novel about Branwell Bronte's barber.

WALLS

This is one of those Southern War stories - you know, a bit fantastic, like that one about the village girl who gave birth to a snake. I can't say how much truth there is in this, but a bit for sure. There were newspaper reports, and even I've seen that photograph of the young girl just hanging there in the trees like an unholy fruit. My Uncle Banjo, he says that she's Nadah, the girl this story happened to. Nadah killed herself for love though, not out of despair at the war, as the news articles made out.

Like the snake-baby yarn, Uncle Banjo tells this as if he'd been there. He fought in that war, swears to the truth of this, so it's mostly his version I'll give you here. When we were children, Banjo used to tell this as if it was a fairy-tale. You know, once upon a time there was a happy ending. But as we grew older, his telling of it became darker. Myself, I don't like all that little-girl-cleaning stuff in the tale, not since I got out of my own despicable marriage last year. But that's a different story. After discussion with my sisters I've decided to leave the household chores in, if only for history's sake. Anyway, the whole thing doesn't hang the same without them.

This all took place in a little border town called Divic, about a hundred kilometers south from the old city of Mahrib. Divic was such a pretty place to look upon. Small, tidy homes stood in rows, terraced up and down the slopes of a curling valley. Brick chimneys uncoiled smoke into the blue sky, and red-tiled roof-tops littered with basking cats glowed in the sunshine. Because of Mahrib's elaborate system of dams and water channels to the north, the surrounding countryside was lush and fertile. Food was abundant in the fields; fat sheep and cattle dotted the hillsides; ripe fruit shone in clusters upon the trees. A perfect place to live and grow up in, had it not been for the spreading of The Southern Wars.

In the town there lived an old man, a carpenter by trade. He had two grown-up sons away fighting in the south, and these boys he'd not seen or heard from for nearly two years. His wife had died some years before. While he worked on jobs around the district or clattered about in his work-shed behind the cottage, the home was kept clean and tidy by his only daughter, the unfortunate Nadah. She was just fifteen at this time, a fragile, beautiful girl, elegant and long legged like a graceful heron. Her skin had the soft whiteness of magnolia flowers. Raven-black hair cascaded over her shoulders, her little face bobbling pretty as an opening bud on a stem. Despite all this beauty, Nadah did have her flaws. Her hands were callused on the palms, wrinkled and hardened from years of washing and cleaning after her father and brothers. And while one of her eyes was blue as a corn-flower, the other was the bright brown of freshly turned earth. As if wanting to draw attention to this oddity, Nature had played a mean trick on her, for she was wall-eyed on her brown side. She was born timid, and these slight defects made her over-shy. Such was her stuttering reluctance to speak with other people that most in the village thought her a simpleton. Others, those of a closed-mind, country mentality, feared her because of her 'ghost-gaze', as they called it. These people could never tell if she was looking at them or through them, and this made many uneasy in her presence. The town bigots and the narrow-minded had labelled her a devil's child, even when she was just a toddling little girl. As she grew older other children, warned against her by their own parents, refused to play with Nadah, and she was mercilessly teased in the streets. Such was the hostility that, as years went on, she rarely left the house. She blossomed through girlhood utterly unaware of her own beauty, of how to make good use of her blessings. Had her mother survived to coax little Nadah out from her dreamy shell, no doubt things would have been different. She would have been the beauty of the district, sought after and wooed by all the eligible men. But poor Nadah, so shy, so lonely, no mother or female friends to turn to. She approached adolescence in a solitary, friendless world, happy enough to carry out chores for her father, content enough with his company and the hazy, warm memories of her mother.

The Southern War exploded from a border skirmish into a major war. With soldiers and bandits from all sides marauding through the area, and Nadah now flowering through puberty, the old carpenter was very much afraid for his daughter. Being a man of his hands, and of a crafty mind, he decided to do something to still his worries, something to ensure his girl's safety should Divic be over-run by the enemy. In secret, working at night with as little noise as possible, he partitioned off a fireside corner of the kitchen with a plasterboard wall to make a secret chamber. The chamber had just enough room for one person to stand upright, and behind the standing space the mouth of a short tunnel led away into a tiny basement room. This room he had dug out beneath his cluttered workshop behind the house, carrying the soil away with him on other jobs, taking care to scatter it far away from the house. So stealthy and careful was he with his secret work that beside himself and Nadah not another soul knew of the hidden basement or partition. Over the months he plumbed in a water tap and ventilation pipes. He hollowed out food-storage space, and even added a toilet well in the corner where the water drained away. Such was his handiwork that not a trace of his construction could be seen from the outside. To tap the kitchen walls they sounded solid, for he had back-spaced with brick, and the entrance hatch was low down beside the chimney stack. Such a skillful job that not even his sons would have spotted the work, had they returned home from the fighting and sat down for a drink in their own kitchen.

On the day the old carpenter was satisfied that his work was completed he called his daughter into the kitchen.

"Now Nadah," he told her. "You've seen what work I've been up to these last months...'

Adèle Geras

Adèle Geras was born in Jerusalem in 1944 and educated at Roedean School, Brighton, and St Hilda's College, Oxford. She has been writing for children and young adults since 1976 and has published more than 70 books, including most recently *Troy* (David Fickling Books). Her collection of poems for adults is called *Voices from the Dolls' House* (Rockingham Press) and she has won several awards for her poetry. She is married with two daughters and lives in Manchester. *Imaginary Furniture* is her work in progress.

From IMAGINARY FURNITURE

INVITATION

This time, be careful.
They have removed all the stones
That you used last time.

I have ironed sheets
and put green pears to blacken
on the bottom shelf

of the oven. Come
alone or with another.
That doesn't matter.

My mouth is open,
all my loose teeth are sharpened
and the cake is baked.

Let's pipe the icing
into red blobs like bloodstains
and call them flowers.

Pull the shutters closed.
We'll lick and suck the white hours
until you ripen.

Follow the thin bird.
Stay in those flapping shadows
and you will be bones.

CARNIVAL

She's been collecting bright things for six months.
Anything she can find: the smallest pearls
glowing faint moonlight, and some satin flames
of ribbon, fire-gold. And silver braid
so dazzling she has to turn away,
and twinkle-twinkle-little-star glass beads.

She shakes her treasures out of paper bags,
chooses with care, then picks the needle up.
Soon, the first sequin, like a tiny sun
glitters and blazes on the taffeta
of her wide skirt, scarlet as Carnival.

TEAPOT

She likes this teapot better than the last.
That one had flowers (pink? She can't recall)
with gold-frilled petals and green stems bound up
in ribbons permanently working loose.
This one has birds, painted the special blue
reserved for oceans, skies and crockery.
They're striding confidently round the pot
on long and glossy legs. They have bright eyes,
breasts feathered white, and small, redundant wings.
Their dark, curved beaks are pointing at the spout.

The tea's the same. She really ought to find
something significant to write about.

GOING TO THE NATIONAL FILM THEATRE

You said: meet me on the other side.
And crossing Hungerford Bridge
it was always twilight:
electric stars switched on in the lilac sky
and the river flat grey or dirty brown
or green like old linoleum.
Never mind. I'll think it into silver -
Spenser's sweet Thames,
which ran, ran softly till the movie ended
and our loud metal footsteps took us back
over the bridge and down to Charing Cross.

THE SUITOR

Mother, on first acquaintance
he is not to my taste.

(Put him in the Yellow Room.
Gather me into my garments.)

His coat glitters like cockroaches.
His boots contain nightmares.

(Pull the flat maids out
from between grey sheets.)

His fingernails are white;
unreasonably curved.

(At eleven o'clock the family portraits
open their mouths to scream.)

Wallpaper absorbs and disperses
the shadow of his hat.

(I am wearing a bustle.
I am wearing a corset.
I am wearing a hat
with a veil; with a black veil.)

Tears leave stains
at the bottom of teacups.
Sighs become cobwebs.

Mother, have you seen them?
Mother, is it rude to speak of them?
There, there, thrusting between his shoulderblades
he has a pair of ribbed and leathery wings.

(He will spread them.
They will mask the light;
groan and flap like an umbrella
in an ecstasy of wind.
They will fall into dry folds
when he is done with them.)

Put him in the Yellow Room.
Let me consider.

WHITE TOWER

There were stairs
on the way up.
I am sure of it.

I can see the wall.
Beyond the wall
there must be something,
but I cannot say
exactly what it is.

There was a door
on the way in.
I am sure of it,

but thorn trees have grown
as quick as weeds
and covered it.

The stairs have melted.
Your footsteps, as you left,
turned them to wax,
which has blocked the stairwell
and set in every crevice.

You have made the tower
your particular candle.
Presently, my hair will flare to gold.

There were other places
before this room.
I am sure of it.

Jane Harris

Jane Harris was Writer in Residence at Durham jail for two years, during which time she compiled *Words from Within: Tales and Experiences of Prison and Prisoners* (Two Heads, 1994). Her novel, *Hollyland*, is the darkly comic story of a 14 year old girl who embarks on a sexual adventure following her mother's death.

From HOLLYLAND

Nel grabbed the doofer and turned the telly down. Then we kicked off our shoes and moved onto the floor. I was feeling pretty sexy by this time. I think Nel was too. He pushed up my Aertex and briefly did fluttery things to me and my nipples with his tongue, some of which were quite nice. But they didn't last long because very quickly he moved his attention to my skirt and knickers. Skirt up, knickers down. Unzip trousers. You could tell he'd done all this before. He was totally agile and everything. Even the plastercast on his arm didn't slow him down. He just worked around it, and guided my hand onto his pants. They were scorching, about the hottest place in the universe. And you could see the shiny end of his knob peeping out the waistband. Knobs. You just don't expect them to be purple.

I rubbed him and patted him, through the material. It reminded me of making baguettes in Domestic Science. I quite got into it. But this bit didn't last long either, apparently, because very quickly we were onto the next stage. Pants off. That was an eye-opener, I can tell you.

"No way that'll get inside me," I said.

"Just c'mere."

"It won't. It takes me about 55 years to get a mini-tampon in."

Nel hesitated. "Have you not done it with anybody yet?"

"No."

He looked sceptical.

"I haven't, honest."

He frowned. Then he blew through his lips and made a noise like a horse.

"Heavy," he said.

"What's heavy about it?" I said. "I'll be fine."

He took a foil-wrapped Durex out his trouser pocket and studied it. Then he held it up in front of my face. "D'you really want to?"

"Uh-huh, but..."

"What?"

His knob swayed up and down a few times – very slowly, like something that was perfectly balanced – almost as if it was giving me the once-over. There was even a slit in the end like a half-shut eye. No, more like a mouth. A miniature mouth.

And the size of it. No question, Nel's knob was a stoater.

I nodded at it. "Is that normal?"

Nel grunted. "What d'you mean normal?" He started tearing open the Durex packet with his teeth.

"I mean, is that normal sized, for a knob?"

Nel looked pleased. "Supposedly not." He admired it himself, with his head on one side. "Supposedly, it's the biggest one anybody's ever seen. All the guys around here say that when it's up, it's like a baby's arm hanging out a pram."

"Guys have seen your erect knob?"

But he didn't answer, because he was rolling the Durex on, and then he was on top, trying to jab himself inside me. The pain was excruciating, like someone trying to shove a collapsed umbrella up between your legs.

"I can't get in," he said, after a minute. "Just relax."

"It's too sore," I told him. "How much is in?"

"A bit. The top bit."

"But how much, in inches?"

"Probably one and a half or something. Let me just try again."

"No, stop. It's agony."

Nel rolled off and leaned on his elbow, looking at me, with this very grumpy expression on his face. Then he peeled off the Durex, and inspected his willie, looking for damage.

I said, "Maybe if I have some more wine I might relax a bit."

"Drink up then," he said and lit himself a fag. I was beginning not to like him so much. But I was determined to look on the bright side. I opened the other bottle.

"If I get dead drunk," I said, "I might not notice anything at all."

"But you're supposed to notice something."

"Have you taken lots of girls' virginitys?"

"Some."

I drank three glasses down, one after the other, while Nel played with his willie. He wasn't masturbating himself exactly. Just fiddling around.

"Watch this," he said. "I'm a ventriloquist."

He pinched the end of his knob between his fingers, making the slit-mouth move, and he put on a squeaky voice.

"What's your name?" the mouth asked.

"Holly," I said. "What's yours?"

The mouth had to think about this for a minute. Then it squeaked, "Algernon."

"Oh, that's nice."

The mouth grinned. "Would you like to give me a kiss?"

"No thanks."

"Just one wee lick?" it squeaked, "Go on."

I shook my head and looked away. After that, nobody said anything for a bit.

Mick Imlah

Mick Imlah was born in Aberdeen in 1956. He read English at Magdalen College, Oxford, where he was subsequently a Junior Fellow. He is currently Poetry Editor at the *Times Literary Supplement*. He has recently co-edited the *New Penguin Book of Scottish Verse*. Author of *Birthmarks* (Chatto, 1989), his next collection, *The Lost Leader*, is in preparation.

---

from THE LOST LEADER

PAST CARING

As a ship
Sees only the tip
Of the ice's pyramid
That has already scraped her bows,
We'd glimpsed that drink was something you overdid;
Now after the wreck I sift the damage you'd stowed
in the house.

Eyes glazed
I fumble, amazed,
Through mounds of knickers and slips,
Extracting the bottles you'd buried there; these
I hump in their binbags, clashing against my knees
To the 'Bottlebank', by the public baths; it takes four trips.

The gin!
No wonder you're thin;
Hundreds of bottles of gin;
And feeding them singly into the ring
My arm grows weary from shifting the bottles of gin;
– A numbing collection of lots of exactly the same thing.

You were vain
As you went down the drain;
Why else would you lay up this hoard
If it wasn't one day to take stock as I'm doing
Of what an almighty amount you had taken on board?
And here am I turning your trophies to scrap at an
illicit viewing!

A smear
Of lipstick, here –
Like the kiss on a valentine;
And sniffing the neck I feel suddenly near to you,
For what it gives off is your smell, if we kissed any time,
And it wasn't a cheap perfume – but the only thing properly
dear to you

Next week
If you're not past caring
They may let you out for an airing,
– To slump in your armchair, too burgled to speak,
The fish out of water that stubbornly stays but the more fish;
– Then how shall we drag the treasure you were back
to the surface?

Julian Barnes

"... you would have to
be exceedingly vain
or exceedingly foolish
to set up as a writer
and think that your
art will sustain you
until death."

Reuben Lane

Reuben Lane was born in Ipswich in 1966. He lives in east London and works as a cinema usher. His short stories have featured in several anthologies (*Random Factor, Does the Sun Rise Over Dagenham?, Pretext*). His first novel, *Throwing Stones at Jonathan,* was published last year by Pulp Books. Reuben's work in progress, *The Dragon Fields*, is a novel of linked stories.

From THE DRAGON FIELDS

WRESTLING WITH ANGELS

Joshua couldn't understand:

"You mean he touched you? Is that what you're saying – The chink?"

"I can't remember – I think so. I was four years old."

Blue removed his make up and put his feet up on the padded seat. End of the day bristles shining on his chin.

My mother only wore make up on Saturday nights when she and my father went to see the greyhounds racing at Catford Stadium.

Blue took me into his caravan and sat me on his lap. All the gossip of our streets started at his loins. He pulled me into his breasts and I was choked with the smell of marzipan that clung to his dress.

We had been to see 'Bedknobs And Broomsticks' at the Gaumont. I wanted a bed like that. A bed that could fly.

Blue's caravan was a sour green on the outside and a milky white inside. He sucked on a cigarette and blew the smoke in my face. He had unloosened his fall of black hair that at the laundry he kept tied up with rubber-bands. He said in Canton they called this plait a kew. I liked saying "Blue's kew."

Blue's caravan was my Saturday night.

I removed my make up. It's been a long night. I've finished, but Joshua is still on his last gent. I imagine – just the other side of the wall – that room filling up with all the spunk that has ever been spilled on the greasy mattress.

The white cream remover feels cold. Dabbing at my cut lip where an off-duty policeman insisted on digging in his teeth; the cotton wool soaking up the cream, the lippie, blood and mascara.

We take a bath together. And then we set off. We're starving. There's an all-night bakery about a mile's walk away where we often go for hot salt-beef bagels dripping with mustard and butter.

My lip still bleeding.

"The bastard." Joshua washed the cut and dowsed it with stinging Dettol.

"Fuck you. It's the kids round here I'm thinking about," the policeman had said doing up his trouser zip. "I've got a son of my own." He pulled a snapshot from the pocket of his wallet and stared at it. Then he bent down and licked up the trickle of blood from where he'd bitten me five minutes earlier. "You lot should be shipped off to some desert island surrounded by a sea full of sharks and piranhas."

We walk through the Victorian squares with their rain-stained verdigris statues and black iron railings. Soot and limestone steps. Past a video shop; the window postered up with all the latest Hindi action flicks. Our stomachs rumbling.

A maroon joint of beef sits in the window on a steel plate under a hot lamp. The women behind the counter know all their regulars by name: trade, cabbies, junkies and insomniacs. Joanie, the woman with the ginger wig, hacks off a chunk of meat for us and smothers it in a spoonful of mustard.

My father would tap at the caravan window with his bunch of keys when they got back from the dogs.

Blue opened the door. And my mother would climb inside – her rouged cheeks and white pallor – unsteady on her Saturday night gold spangly heels. She'd hoik up the hem of her dress and kneel beneath the table and lean in – I'd always be awake but I'd pretend to be fast asleep – her breath smelling like Christmas pudding – and she'd whisper "Have you been a good boy then?" And turning to look over her shoulder: "He hasn't been naughty has he Blue?" And Blue would click his tongue – the way he did. And her voice was always hoarse. She told Blue how much they had won – how she'd a hunch on such and such a hound – screaming herself silly as it chased the hare around the last bend. And Blue would ask "Won't you both stop for a cup of tea?" And my mother would say "Thank you – But we're witnessing in the morning." Her arms crept between me and the canvas and she lifted me and carried me out to the back of our Hillman Imp. Father, who never came inside the caravan, already at the wheel, revving the engine.

Sprawled on Joshua's chest. His voice deep from lack of sleep. Holding me before I spill away.

James Poyser

James Poyser has written a novel, *In a Lonely Place*, (Hamish Hamilton, 1991); a play, *The Idol on the Bronze Horse*, performed at Contact Theatre, Manchester, and Palace of Creativity, St Petersburg, 1994; and a radio series, *Stockport, So Good They Named It Once*, which has just finished on Radio 4 with a new series out in the autumn. His current novel is *Dance Hall at Louse Point* – a story of doomed love.

From DANCE HALL AT LOUSE POINT

February was the coldest since records began and to ward off the inclemency of the season, not to mention the inclemency of my life in general, I went into a kind of moral hibernation. I was like a tortoise, in a cardboard box stuffed with straw. Someone had put me in the cool garage a few weeks back and I just lay there, my heart beating three times a minute. People seemed strange to me, as I imagine people do seem strange to a tortoise. I didn't really know who they were. I didn't know what they wanted. Of me, in particular.

Take Caroline. She rang me, a few days after Danny's party. She was back in Sunderland. There was no prospect of us meeting. But even so, there were things I should have said to her, words of kindness, of reassurance, even of thanks. But I said hardly a word. I felt sort of punch drunk, like there were thoughts in my brain somewhere, floating around in the soupy mush of my consciousness, but I just couldn't fish them out, let alone array them neatly into meaningful utterances.

I read once about a man who became so disconnected, so dislocated from the world that one night he awoke to find a three foot long fleshy trunk-like creature in his bed which he attacked with great vehemence only to realise the following morning that it was his own leg. Well it was kind of like that with Caroline calling me. *Jamais Vu*, I think you might call it. I knew who she was, I knew what she was talking about. Indeed, I remembered everything. But I recognised nothing. Everything was somehow distorted, and by the time it hit whatever part of the brain is in charge of understanding what the fuck's going on, the signal was down.

I spoke to her twice, I think. A third time she left a message on the answerphone. I was in when she left it, but I didn't pick up and though I listened to what she said, it seemed strangely irrelevant, like it was being left not for me but for some non-existent flatmate whose private life didn't interest me very much.

She didn't ring again.

As for Emily, well, I thought about her. But she too was fading, sinking slowly into that foreign land which is the past. She was nearing the border now, where reality meets memory. She had her passport at the ready (with that stupid photo of her with her hair up and that slightly haunted look in her eyes as though she'd been chased all the way to the photo booth by wolves).

That month I immersed myself in work. Like some Gogolian penpusher I actually began to enjoy the trivial minutiae of my job. My boss Eric and my workmates - tall Julie and short Julie - became at first worried by my behaviour but then enthused and even strangely elated when they realised that, so cut off was I, they could give me *anything* to do and I wouldn't object.

"So," said short Julie. "One of us has to go to the World Lager Fair and one of us has to read this four-hundred page report called 'Attitudes to Cheese'. How are we going to divide this up, Mike?"

As if I hadn't really heard the question I replied in a vague, dreamy mutter.

"I'll read the report."

And I did. All of it. I lost myself for a week in a

world of cheese - the enigma of double Gloucester, the in-fridge profile of soft cheese - where there were no people, no ex-girlfriends, no best friend's sisters. Nobody. Just cheese. And cheese was simple. Cheese was easy. If the world around me could be cheese, I thought, then my problems here would be swiftly at an end.

I travelled a lot at that time, all in the name of market research. I went to Glasgow to talk to teenagers about tracksuits; I toured around Lincolnshire talking to farmers about cereal herbicides; in Kent I discussed the cost of electricity with many shopkeepers.

I even went to Belgium. To canvas opinion, in my piss-poor French, on a new type of industrial cloth-tape.

I tell you. A man can really lose himself in Belgium.

They say people work to live. At that time I was working to forget about life. I was a zombie in a nice suit. A member of the undead, but keeping more regular hours and staying in more Novotels. I hardly went out. Even when I was back in London. I just couldn't be arsed. I kept the flat tidy, washed my clothes, ate functionally. I watched a season of Frank Sinatra films BBC2 was running. I didn't really like any of them.

Leone Ross

Leone Ross is a novelist and short story writer. She has written two novels, *All the Blood is Red*, and *Orange Laughter*, due for US publication in 2000. Her work will also appear in the Warner anthology, *Dark Matter* in July 2000. *Faith is Seven* is her third novel. It tells the story of the strangely gifted Faith, who is hunted for her ability to change human perception of the world.

From FAITH IS SEVEN

Faith was determined to watch. She placed the bowl of ackee on the kitchen table, slipped out of the front door, and tiptoed to the side of the house where balancing on a helpful rock gave her a full view of the bedroom where her brothers stood facing each other.

Dante reached up and placed his small, cupped hands over Eliot's ears. His aura was green as the sea grapes that washed up in fat, damp bunches on the island's shore. Eliot smiled. His aura was red, a shifting, changing cloak that moved from blood to wine to lightest pink, depending on his mood. But as Dante touched him, it disappeared.

Faith blinked. She had never seen anyone without colour before. But as quickly as it disappeared, another came, a deep olive that seemed to dive into Eliot through Dante's hands and spread through his body. Eliot jumped, but his mother's voice stilled him.

"What do you see, Eliot?" she said.

"Water..." Eliot's voice was hushed.

"Tell me about the water."

"It's so pretty..."

"What kind of water is it?"

"It's the sea...it's so big, so big——!"

"Look into the water," said Dante. His eyes were closed, his body very still. "Just look. And be the water."

Faith's knees suddenly felt so weak that she sat down, small dust clouds rising around her, her backside hurting where it chafed against the rock. A headache began to throb at her left temple. She put her palm against the wall of the house and tried to get up, but her hand seemed to disappear into the cement, and she went down again, hitting the ground but not feeling it. Her mind was filling with something new, something so insistent and overwhelming that her body jerked in fear. She could not have felt her skin now if she had tried. It had all flowed away, taken over by rushing, rushing liquid. She opened her mouth and tried to form the word that sank, dimly, into the onslaught of the merciless ocean: *stop*, but the water poured on, unheeding.

Strawberry jolted out of the concentration she'd focussed on her sons.

Something else was happening.

"*Be water*," urged Dante.

Faith writhed in the dust. The roar of the waves was unmistakable. She could feel them lapping over her, no, there was no her, no beginning, no end, no little girl. Only the song of the terrible sea. Soon she would be gone, and as the thought struggled for consideration, she felt the promise of an overwhelming peace.

Be the sea.

Be the water.

It would be nice.

"Faith?" Strawberry opened her bedroom door. The kitchen was empty, bowls deserted. She stood still, listening, stretching out for her child's presence. "*Faith*!" she yelled. There was no answer. She whirled around as Jason burst through the kitchen door, legs pumping, breathless. Yes. Jason would know.

"*She's drowning*!" he yelled.

She grabbed his arms. "Where is she?"

"I don't know! Daddy's gone down to the pier!"

Strawberry ran.

Faith was almost gone. As Dante gave Eliot the gift of the sea's beauty, he filled his sister's lungs with water, choking her, great sprays of liquid spewing from her lips. She opened her eyes, and salt water poured down her face. It was the sting of salt that saved her life. The ocean tore at her eyeballs, slamming her back into a moment's consciousness, long enough to hear her father calling her from where he dove and splashed and searched the Caribbean Sea. Faith snapped her neck back and began to fight her brother. Her mind reached for a single word.

Dry.

The force of her push was enough to send Dante and Eliot reeling away from each other. Strawberry looked up into the sky as the pipes across the island exploded. There was a flurry of activity as tourists opened doors and called out in concern and fear. The sea shrank from Christopher and Jason's feet, baring a new shoreline as if some great plug had been pulled in the firmament. A flock of parrots dropped from their perch on a nearby tree, their blood coagulated. Strawberry felt her throat begin to constrict. She turned to her husband. He was struggling to get to his feet, clutching at his chest. She watched Jason pause in the sudden, arid wind, concentrating, and then watched him turn his head towards the house, wordless through the dry heat of his mouth.

Strawberry began to run up the sandbank, screaming her daughter's name, ignoring the knives cutting into her lungs as birds showered around her.

Hanif Kureishi

"What most writers
need more than
anything, apart from
inspiration, is time
and that is an
expensive
commodity."

Henry Shukman

Henry Shukman wrote his first book, *Sons of the Moon*, at the age of nineteen. A recent winner of the *Times Literary Supplement* Poetry Prize, he has published poetry in *London Magazine, Stand* and *The Iowa Review*. His fiction has appeared in the *Hudson Review*, the *Missouri Review*, the *New England Review* and *O.Henry Prize Stories 1999. Mortimer of the Maghreb* is his work in progress.

From MORTIMER OF THE MAGHREB

Ibrahim grinned at Mortimer and whispered, "I could pick them off with my Kalashnikov from here."

Mortimer believed him. He and Ibrahim lay side by side at the top of a mound, passing a pair of binoculars back and forth. Ahead of them, perhaps two hundred yards away, the top halves of three Moroccan soldiers showed as little figures above a long, low dune. This was the third time in one day that Mortimer had been asked to crawl up a stony bank to peer at Moroccan positions. He was tiring of it. He couldn't write a story about looking at soldiers.

And it was uncomfortable. Little stones pricked his elbows and knees.

He nodded at Ibrahim and began to move down the slope. Ibrahim immediately started too, so that the initiative might seem his.

Back at the camp, Mortimer wrote: *the noisiest place on earth is not a pressing mill, not a rave, not an aircraft test hangar, but a war. War assaults not the ears but the bones.*

He closed his notebook. He was lying. This war was quiet. Now and then came the soft thud of a shell exploding far away, well off target, its sound absorbed by the endless desert. The enemy had installed a radar artillery system at immense cost and to little effect.

Mortimer had forgotten the strange matter-of-factness of war, the way you could be in the heart of a war and not even know it. Nothing really happened. You just drove about in an empty landscape. You saw no one. Occasionally you heard a distant boom, but otherwise nothing told you a war was going on. Except for something in the men, perhaps, a calmness born of danger, as if you could tell they were saving themselves for something big.

Several times on his first day Mortimer heard the distant thud-thud of the Moroccan artillery, followed a few seconds later by a pair of brief whines, two soft crashes. The guerrillas had long since learnt to dodge the radar. Ibrahim pointed out a faint stick on the horizon once, between two hills. "Radar antenna," he said.

Mortimer nodded and felt he ought to take a picture, but buckled up in his jacket and headscarf, it seemed like too much trouble.

In the evening and all the second day they travelled on the terrain Mortimer remembered. It was an amazing land, a rolling plain of gravel - real gravel, like on a drive in Hampshire or Connecticut. It went on for hundreds of miles. In the morning it looked like a beaten sheet of silver. At noon it shimmered like overheated metal. In the late afternoon, golden light hovered above it, blinding like the ocean. And for ten minutes just after the sun slipped down, it wheeled itself through the entire spectrum, beginning with a fiery red, ending in luminous violet. Under the moon it glittered like sugar.

A.L. Kennedy

It is good if writing is not always carried out in a rarefied atmosphere, but the silencing of all but our nation's strongest and already most often represented voices by economic pressures is our loss."

Atima Srivastava

Atima Srivastava was born in Mumbai, India, and moved to London at the age of eight. She has written two novels, *Transmission* and *Looking for Maya* (Quartet). She has been Writer in Residence at the University of Singapore and the University of Sophia (Bulgaria). She has won first prize in the Bridport Arts Short Story competition, an Arts Council Award for her second novel, and a Hawthornden Fellowship. She has worked in television for over 13 years as a film editor and, more recently, as a director. She lives in north London. *Stanley and Other Stories* is her work in progress.

From STANLEY AND OTHER STORIES

No one at the Post Office knew he'd fallen down on the slippery floor. He had lain there for hours before the supervisor found him, moaning to himself in agony. The hospital didn't like talking to us and couldn't understand my mum's English. The doctor got irritated when my mother didn't understand what a stroke was. He explained that my dad couldn't use his limbs anymore and his speech would be slurred. She was suspicious. She thought they'd done something to him in hospital: how could a fall, a simple fall from a stepladder, do all this damage? But it had. My dad came home a vegetable.

He used to cry all the time. After school, I would make us both a cup of tea and start cooking the evening meal. Sometimes, my dad would sit at the Formica kitchen table and watch me fry up cumin seeds, careful not to burn myself. My mother had warned me. No one else would be able to run the house if I was careless and burnt myself and got myself into hospital. Other times, he would walk himself slowly into the other room and sit in front of the television watching the repeats from the morning. There was a limit to what he could talk to a ten-year old about, even if he could talk. He went to physiotherapy twice a week - the bus came to collect him - but those days he seemed more depressed. He couldn't do it. He was ashamed at having to go. He didn't like the therapy; it made him realise how helpless he was. White people were different, being independent was in their blood; they were brought up like that. Us Indians, he'd say, we were fatalistic. God had meant it to happen; there was no point in trying to change your destiny.

Although my mum had a little shrine in her bedroom where she prayed every morning after her bath and lit incense, she wasn't the kind of woman to let God have his way. She asked for the hardest shifts at work, did the longest hours, saved every penny, shrunk her face into a skeleton. It was a few months before she realised she could have claimed compensation, but it was too late now. She slapped me across the face when I put too much salt in the Dahl and we had to throw it away. We had to manage, she knew we had to manage. She told him to swallow his pride and queue up at the social security office to claim his disability benefit. At night, I could hear her fighting with him when he could hardly speak. No one was going to help us. The Post Office, all those friends he'd had there, none of them had told us about the compensation. The supervisor sent a little basket of flowers with a get well soon card stuck in it.

They used to call my dad Jay there; they wouldn't pronounce Jaideep. It was a common name in India, especially in the Gujerat where he came from. He had gone to Kenya to work as a clerk in the railways as a young man and married there. My mother's family couldn't afford to support them when I came along and I was brought over to India as a baby, to live in my grandparents' house. I explained to Stanley how it wasn't a terrible thing to do; it happened to a lot of kids. Grandparents in Indian society weren't considered outsiders. In any case, I knew nothing of genealogy. My ancestral home was like a heaven. I spent my childhood playing on the swings in the backyard, being pampered by everybody who all thought I was something special with my big eyes. The women of the house would sit on the verandah, one after the other, as if we were in a canoe. Each checking the other's head for lice and rubbing jasmine oil into the scalp. I was at the end of the row and would wriggle away, running about gleefully but, although they scolded me, no one could contain my exuberance. The man I assumed to be my father would offer me his hand, make me promise to hold on tight as we weaved around the open-air vegetable market full of yellow, red and brown spice hills on flattened hessian sacks. The hollering vendors gave respectful salaams to my guardian. All of them seemed to know where we lived. It was a big house with trees and goats and chickens and as far as I knew we were as rich as kings. The day my mother arrived to take me back was the worst day of my life.

Jackie Wullschlager

Jackie Wullschlager was born in 1962 and educated at Oxford. She is literary critic and European Arts Correspondent for the *Financial Times*, and the author of *Inventing Wonderland* (Methuen,1995), a multiple biography of Victorian and Edwardian children's writers. Her next book will be *Hans Christian Andersen: The Life of a Storyteller.*

From HANS CHRISTIAN ANDERSEN: THE LIFE OF A STORYTELLER

INTRODUCTION

Hans Christian Andersen was a compulsive autobiographer. At school, he says, "I told the boys curious stories in which I was always the chief person, but was sometimes ridiculed for that." He wrote his first memoir in 1832, when he was twenty-seven, and published a new autobiography for every decade of his adult life – in 1847, 1855 and 1869. The gulf between his childhood as the son of an illiterate washerwoman, and his career as a writer famous across Europe, the confidante of monarchs and princes, prompted constant self-review. Throughout his writings you can hear him gasping for breath as his high connections sweep him off his feet. "Twenty-five years ago I arrived with my small parcel in Copenhagen, a poor stranger of a boy, and today I have drunk my chocolate with the Queen, sitting opposite her and the King at the table", he wrote in 1844.

But his best-known self-portraits, inventive, harsh, spiritually true, are in his fairy tales. He is the triumphant Ugly Duckling and the loyal Little Mermaid, the steadfast Tin Soldier and the king-loving Nightingale, the demonic Shadow, the depressive Fir Tree, the forlorn Little Matchgirl. These are the stories which made Andersen a household name, and give him a place in literary history as one of the greatest and most original of European writers.

His importance as a creator of fairy tales is immense. While before him a few authors – Charles Perrault in France, the Grimm brothers in Germany – collected folk tales recounted by oral lore, Andersen was the first writer to treat this peasant form as a literary genre and to invent new tales which entered the collective consciousness with the same mythic power as the ancient, anonymous ones. Almost two hundred years after Andersen wrote them, stories such as "The Emperor's New Clothes" and "The Ugly Duckling" remain bywords for aspects of the human condition, while characters epitomising terror or sacrifice, such as the Snow Queen or the Little Mermaid, are as deeply imbedded in our culture as those from traditional folklore like "Cinderella" or "Sleeping Beauty".

Andersen's miniaturist universe encompasses the full scope of human frailty and grandeur of spirit....

He wrought from the fairy tale his own art, pouring into it his compulsion to understand and mythologise his own life, transforming the emptiness and pain he felt into artistic order. Any random object, it appeared, would do as an alter ego – a soldier or a snowman, but also a spinning top or a darning needle. "I have heaps of material, more than for any other kind of writing; it often seems to me as if every hoarding, every little flower is saying to me, 'Look at me, just for a moment, and then my story will go right into you, and then, if I feel like it, I have the story," he said.

The autobiographical imperative driving his tales, their honesty to experience, consoles, amuses, enlightens us as we try to make sense of our own lives. For Andersen, that honesty in his art was especially hard-won, for his social and sexual traumas made him in life a man of secrets, repressions and half-truths. Only when he discovered the literary genre of the fairy tale did he find a medium whose formal distance from reality allowed him to write as he was and felt. Addressing himself to the child in the adult through a revolutionary shift in perspective, he gave voice through these characters to groups which had traditionally been mute and oppressed – children, the poor, those who did not fit social or sexual stereotypes. Introducing fantasy and comedy as the key veins, he determined the course of children's literature, suffusing his popular domestic settings with the fatalism of legend and with his own modern sense of the absurd.

Yet two centuries after his birth, Andersen is still not appreciated as the world-class author that he undoubtedly was, as towering and representative a figure of the European romantic spirit as Balzac or Victor Hugo... I hope I have shown how much Andersen has to offer an adult audience, and conveyed some of the struggle against both circumstances and liabilities of temperament – wild imagination, inner rage, tormenting anxieties and hypochondria, insatiable ambition – that formed him. He is a writer of whom one never tires, who grows in depth and maturity with his readers, whose sense of the adventure of life is infinite.

Diran Adebayo

Creative writing strikes me as being, in these fluff-and-instant-orientated times, one of the few remaining areas where you can give people and truths the commitment they deserve. Awards like these, money apart, help to fuel the writer with the self-belief and the stubbornness he or she will surely need.

THE JUDGES

Anne Fine

Anne Fine is a distinguished writer for children of all ages, with over 40 books to her credit. She is twice winner of the Carnegie Medal, Britain's most coveted children's literature award, and has also won The Guardian Children's Literature Award, the Whitbread Children's Novel Award twice, and a Smarties Prize. She won the Publishing News Children's Author of the Year Award in 1990 and again in 1993. An adaptation of her novel *Goggle-Eyes* has been shown by the BBC, and Twentieth Century Fox filmed her novel *Madame Doubtfire* as *Mrs Doubtfire*, starring Robin Williams. Her work has been translated into twenty five languages.

Anne Fine has also written for adults. Her novels *The Killjoy, Taking the Devil's Advice, In Cold Domain* and most recently, *Telling Liddy*, have been published to considerable critical acclaim.

Anne Fine has two grown-up daughters, and lives in County Durham.

Alan Hollinghurst

Alan Hollinghurst was born in 1954. He read English at Magdalen College, Oxford, and subsequently taught there and at University College. He is an admired poet and critic; his critically acclaimed verse translation of Racine's *Bajazet* was published by Chatto in 1992. His novels *The Swimming Pool Library* (1988), *The Folding Star* (1994 shortlisted for the Booker Prize) and *The Spell* (1999) are published by Vintage.

Andrew Motion

Andrew Motion was born in London in 1952 and educated at University College, Oxford. He is Professor of Creative Writing at the University of East Anglia and was appointed Poet Laureate in 1999. He had his first volume of poetry, *The Pleasure Steamers*, published in 1978. In 1994 he won the Whitbread Prize for Biography for his biography of Philip Larkin, *A Writer's Life* and he also published a biography of Keats in 1997. He has published two novels, *The Pale Companion* in 1989 and *Famous for the Creatures* in 1991, and seven volumes of poetry, including *Love in a Life* (1991), *The Price of Everything* and *Salt Water* (1997). He is Chair of the Arts Council Literature Panel and a Fellow of the Royal Society of Literature.

Michèle Roberts

Most writers are poor. Few writers can earn a living just from publishing books. It is scandalous that writers earn royalties at such a low percentage. Given this situation, writers desperately need the Arts Council's Awards. They deserve them. Thanks to the Arts Council for caring enough about Literature to make these awards.